I0766296

Ferenc Margitics

Subjective Well-Being, Individual Aspirations and Spirituality

Subjective Well-Being, Individual Aspirations and Spirituality

Authored by: Ferenc Margitics PhD
(margitics.ferenc@nye.hu)
Edited and published by: Ervin K. Kery
(editor@kery.org)

www.consciousnessbooks.cf

CONTENTS

Preface

The spirituality is part of the life of a great many people, values that play an important role in, among other aspects, leading a healthful life and preserving their health.

In the past fifteen or twenty years, there has been considerable research into the effects of spirituality on people's physical and mental health.

In the course of our research, we examined the level of subjective well-being among college students and the personal individual aspirations of college students.

One of the objectives of our research was to find whether the subjective well-being of students with a higher degree of Spiritual Consciousness was also higher or not.

We intended to survey the differences in personal aspirations between students with a high and those with a low level of Spiritual Consciousness. Efforts were also made to find differences between the genders in people with a high level of Spiritual Consciousness.

Subjective Well-Being and Spirituality

Introduction

The concept of subjective well-being is extremely complex, and the approaches various experts use are also varied. Diener arranges the recent approaches into three groups (Urban, 1995):

> The first type of theories contains those that follow the footsteps of antique thinkers and philosophers and regard subjective well-being as the possession of positive characteristic features and/or emotions that are based upon the fulfillment and activation of personal ambitions and will lead to self-expression and self-implementation.

> The second category contains the so-called top-down models, emphasizing the role of personality and the interpretation of life experience in the definition of subjective well-being. In these theories subjective well-being is

identified with satisfaction with life, which is based upon subjective value judgments and is closely related to the evaluative and attributive functions of the personality.

> The third group of theories is the one that includes the subjective, bottom-up approaches. These theories consider subjective well-being as the summary of pleasure experienced by the person concerned. An individual is happy after, and as a result of, gathering a large number of positive emotions, moods and happy moments.

Today it is obvious that it is necessary to integrate the various theories, as any one of the approaches above in itself will not be suitable for the interpretation of the complex issue of subjective well-being.

According to recent research, it is possible to describe subjective well-being with three major factors (Urban, 1995):

> A level of satisfaction with life as a whole, referring to a cognitive judgment system, with which the individual evaluates his/her life in an overall way.

> Frequency and intensity of positive emotions/affectivity—pleasure and happiness.

> The relative scarcity of negative emotions, depression, fear, anxiety, sadness and other negative situations.

The fact that the individual factors—pleasant emotions, satisfaction with life, negative emotions—are separate and independent of each other has been justified by several surveys (Diener et al., 1999).

Although formerly it was believed that positive and negative emotions were located on the opposing ends of the same axis, today it is regarded as proven that the levels of positive and negative emotions within one individual are relatively independent of each other. There is evidence suggesting that separate neurological operations are responsible for pleasant and unpleasant emotions (Diener, 2000).

Diener (2000) asserts that subjective well-being has several clearly discernible components: satisfaction with life; satisfaction with various parts with life, e.g., job, marriage; the high levels of positive emotions (pleasant experiences and moods) and the low level of negative emotions (unpleasant experiences and moods).

Initial research projects into subjective well-being examined the connections between the personality and happiness, seeking an answer to questions as to whether long-lasting happiness as a feature of the personality exists or whether there are personal characteristic features that are closely related to happiness. Several research programmes suggest that certain characteristic features such as extraversion show a positive correlation with well-being (Lu et al., 1997), whereas neuroticism has a negative effect on personal happiness (Brebner et al., 1995).

Personal characteristic features, however, only explain approximately 30% of the variance (Chan and Joshep, 2000), so the question is still open as to what other specific factors are responsible for subjective well-being.

New tendencies in psychology emerging in the late eighties and early nineties offered new possibilities for measuring subjective well-being and subjective satisfaction with life. The new psychological approaches tend to place more emphasis on personal endeavours (Emmons 1986), personal objectives (Brunstein, 1993) and individual aspirations and strivings (Kassel and Ryan 1993, 1996).

These new research trends draw inspiration from the work of humanistic theoreticians like Rogers, Maslow and Fromm, who believe that our decisions regarding important things in life, what we do in order to achieve our objectives and how we utilize our internal potentials are the decisive factors in our personal subjective well-being.

We believe that our life is sensible and valuable if and when our objectives are congruent with our internal selves, and we are committed to reach our goals, thus improving our personality.

Research Hypotheses

Our initial research hypotheses were the following:

1. There are no differences in the level of subjective well-being between the two genders (Diener et al., 1999).

2. The subjective well-being of students characterized by a higher degree of Spiritual Consciousness is higher than that of students with a lower level of Spiritual Consciousness.

3. There are no gender differences among students with a high degree of Spiritual Consciousness in terms of subjective well-being.

4. Spiritual Consciousness shows a close correlation with certain indicators of subjective well-being.

Methodology

Participants

Data was collected among students at the University of Nyíregyháza.

We collected data randomly at every faculty, and participation was voluntary and done with their consent.

Nine hundred students took part in the research and 854 of them provided valuable data (552 women and 302 men).

The average age was 20,23 (standard deviation 1,51) the median value was 20 years.

Measures

Examination of Subjective Well-Being

Diener's Life Satisfaction Scale

Diener (2000) asserts that subjective well-being is an indicator of how individuals evaluate their lives from cognitive and affective aspects. Individuals make judgments about their lives as a whole and about various parts of the whole, e. g. work, family, marriage etc. In this way, subjective well-being has several components independent of each other. The scale measures the cognitive factor and global satisfaction with live with the help of five statements. Respondents marked the validity of the statements for their particular life on a seven-grade Likert-scale.

The Hungarian version of the scale was successfully used by Martos et al. (2006) in their research programme. They found the reliability of the scale excellent (Cronbach-alpha=0,890).

Bern Subjective Well-Being Inventory

Grob(1995) describes two dimensions of subjective well-being: satisfaction and "ill existence."

The four components of satisfaction are a positive attitude to life, a positive self-esteem, the lack of depressive mood and pleasures in life. Positive attitude towards life means, on the one hand, that the individual has a generally positive approach to life and, on the other hand, that the person is convinced that he or she lives a meaningful life.

Depressive mood means the lack of energy, sadness and withdrawal. The lack of depressive mood is an important indicator of subjective well-being, of satisfaction with life. Pleasures in life mean a positive evaluation and appreciation of human existence, as well as the acceptance of one's personal abilities and characteristics. The two components of "ill existence" are personal problems on the one hand, and the somatic symptoms and reactions on the other.

Personal problems include to what extent a person is preoccupied and annoyed by various problems. Personal problems also include how the individual recognizes and accepts the problems that crop up in their direct social environment as well as how sensitive the individual is to the problematic situations. Somatic symptoms and reactions mean the ability of the individual to convert his or her inner tensions into somatic symptoms.

The questionnaire developed by Grob contains the following dimensions:

- ➢ A positive attitude towards life
- ➢ Personal problems

> ➢ Somatic symptoms and reactions
> ➢ Self-esteem
> ➢ Depressive mood
> ➢ Pleasure in life

Respondents are requested to mark on a seven-grade Likert scale to what extent a statement applies to them.

The Hungarian adaptation of the questionnaire was done by Sallay (2004), who found the reliability of the scales good (Cronbach-alpha=0,69-0,81).

Examination of Spiritual Consciousness

The Spiritual Consciousness Scale (Margitics, 2019)

Following the teachings of Eckhart Tolle, the author created the Spiritual Consciousness Scale (SCS) and carried out its statistical analysis. The purpose has been developing a new measuring instrument for the recognition of spiritual consciousness.

The questionnaire describes the following dimensions of Spiritual Consciousness:

> ➤ Transcending the Functions of Ego
> ➤ Ego-Dyastole (reduction in the functions of Ego)
> ➤ Alert Consciousness in the Present

The Criteria of Compiling the Research Group and the Control Group

For the composition of the examination groups, the results scored on the Spiritual Consciousness Scale.

Students were arranged according to their poisition of the Spiritual Consciousness Scale.

Students low on the Spiritual Consciousness Scale were in the first quarter, whereas those who were high on the scale were put in the fourth quarter (Chart 1).

	Quartiles	
	first	Third
Spiritual Consciousness Scale	52	61

Chart 1. The quartiles of Spiritual Consciousness Scale

The group of low spiritual consciousness created according to the Spiritual Consciousness Scale consisted of 221 individuals (143 women, 78 men); that with a high spiritual consciosness consisted of 214 people (137 women and 77 men).

Results

The descriptive and comparative statistics of the findings achieved with Diener's Life Satisfaction Scale and the Bern Subjective Well-Being Inventory are provided (for the whole of the sample and in a breakdown according to the two genders) in Chart 2.

In order to make the figures comparative, the average values and dispersions are set to one answer on the scale.

	Total (n=854)		Women (n=552)		Men (n=302)	
	Mean	St d.	Mean	St d.	Mean	St d.
Diener's Satisfaction with Life Scale	4,3	1,3	4,3	1,2	4,4	1,3

Bern Subjective Well-Being Questionnaire: Positive attitude towards life	3,5	0,6	3,5	0,6	3,5	0,7
Bern Subjective Well-Being Questionnaire: Personal problems	2,8	0,8	2,8	0,9	2,7	0,7
Bern Subjective Well-Being Questionnaire: somatic symptoms and reactions	2,2***	0,7	2,2	0,7	1,9	0,8
Bern Subjective Well-Being	4,4	0,9	4,4	0,8	4,5	0,9

Questionnaire: Self-esteem						
Bern Subjective Well-Being Questionnaire: Depressive mood	2,1	0,7	2,1	0,7	2,2	0,7
Bern Subjective Well-Being Questionnaire: Pleasure of life	3,5	0,7	3,5	0,6	3,4	0,7

*p<0,05; **p<0,01; ***p<0,001.

Chart 2. The descriptive and comparative statistics of Diener's Life Satisfaction Scale and the Bern Subjective Well-Being Inventory

When examining university students' satisfaction with life, Diener et al. (1999) measured an average of 4,7 (dispersion=1,28). In our college students, we found a value somewhat lower than that; our findings approximately match a medium value on Likert's scale.

Out of Grob's satisfaction index, students scored the highest values in self-esteem, followed by positive attitude towards life and pleasures of life, with almost the same figures. The low scores on the scale of depressive mood is an indicator of the lack of depressive mood.

The indicators of Grob's "ill existence" were low, with the indicators of personal problems somewhat higher than those of somatic reactions. These values—as matched to Likert's five-grade scale—suggest a high level of self-esteem, a somewhat above-the-average level of the positive attitude to life and pleasures of life, an average level of personal problems, and levels below the average in somatic symptoms and depressive mood.

Sallay (2004) conducted a survey among adolescents and found similar values, except in self-esteem (average=1,96, dispersion=0,67), where their figure was lower and in depressive mood (average=3,68, dispersion=0,71) where their figure was higher. These differences are explained by the changes of the adolescent age, and the sample we examined was not characterized by these deviations.

A comparative statistical analysis of the two genders shows any considerable difference between men and women in the somatic symptoms and reactions only. Women appear to be more susceptible to such reactions than men (t=3,856, p<0,003).

Figure 1 contains the descripritive statistics of the results of Diener's Life Satisfaction Scale, employed in the groups arranged according to the Spiritual Consciousness Scale.

The chart suggests that students, regardless of their gender, who achieved a higher score on the Spiritual Consciousness Scale reported a higher degree of subjective well-being than those students who did not possess a high level of Spiritual Consciousness. According to the comparative statisatical analysis (two-sample t-test), the difference is of significant degree (t=8,003, p<0,000).

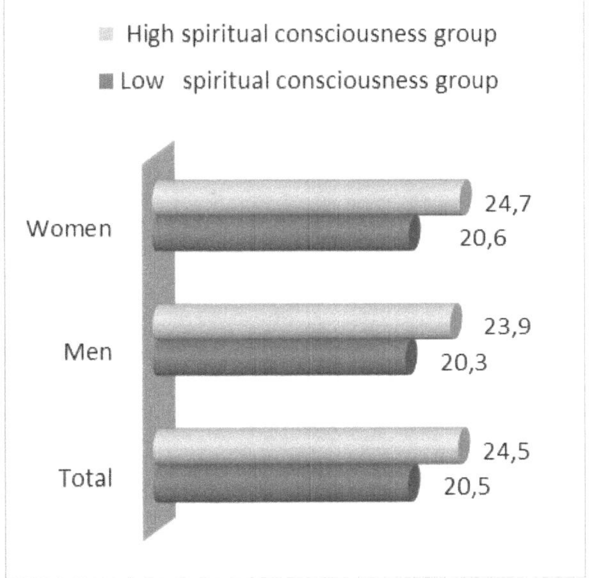

Figure 1. These are the average results the students in the examination groups created according to the Spiritual Consciousness Scale scored on Diener's Life Satisfaction Scale.

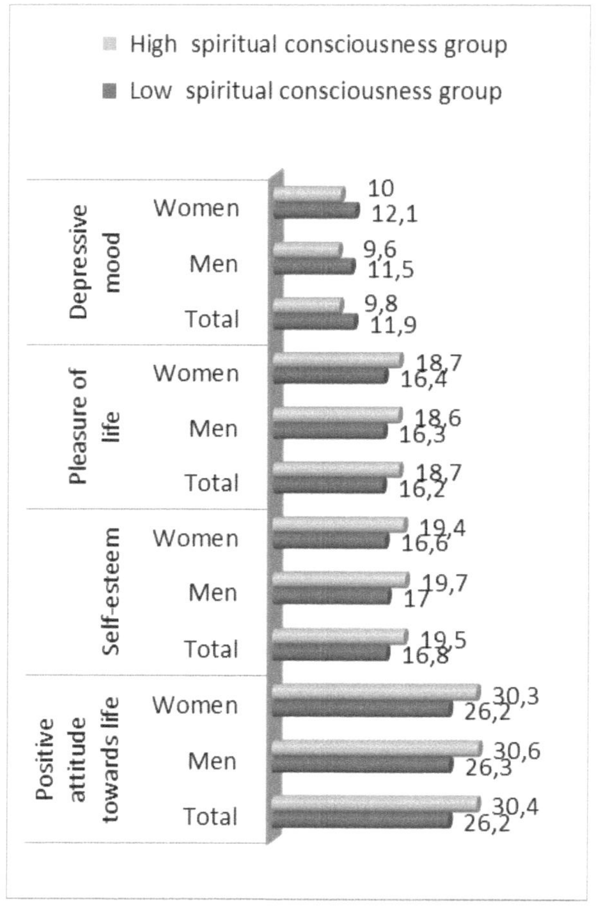

Figure 2. These are the average results the students in the examination groups created according to the Spiritual Consciousness Scale scored on the Bernese Subjective Well-Being Inventory.

Figure 2 contains the descripritive statistics of the results of the Bernese Subjective Well-Being Inventory (positive attitude to life, self-evaluation, pleasures in life, lack of depressive moods) employed in the groups arranged according to the Spiritual Consciousness Scale.

The chart suggests that students, regardless of their gender, who achieved a higher score on the Spiritual Consciousness Scale reported a higher degree of subjective well-being in the Bernese Subjective Well-Being Inventory than those students who did not possess a high level of Spiritual Consciousness (Positive attitude towards life: t=8,925, p<0,000; Self-esteem: t=7,287, p<0,000; Pleasure of life: t=6,925, p<0,000; Depressive mood: t=6,325, p<0,000).

Using Grob's "Disease Existence" indicators, we found that students with a Spiritual Consciousness reported considerably fewer somatic complaints and symptoms (t=2,459, p<0,014) and fewer personal problems (t=2,625, p<0,004) than students who scored lower on the Spiritual Consciousness Scale (Figure 3).

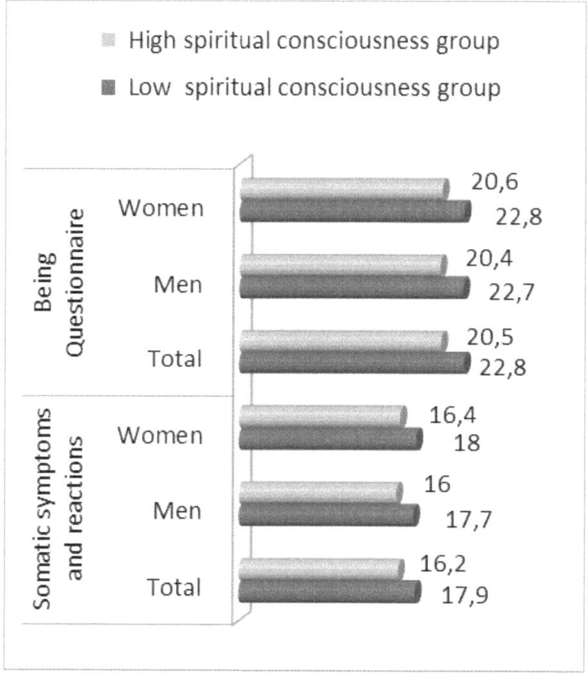

Figure 3. These are average results the students arranged in the examination groups according to the Spiritual Consciousness Scale scored on the Bernese Subjective Well-Being Inventory.

In the following part of the survey, we carried out a linear regression analysis (stepwise method) for the whole of the sample and for each gender separately to analyse the various components of subjective well-being.

Prediktor	β	t	p<
Total: $F_{totál}$=30,442; df=4/854; p<0,000			
Pleasure of life	0,0318	5,930	0,000
Positive attitude towards life	0,310	6,834	0,000
Depressive mood	-0,264	-3,827	0,000
Personal prob-lems	-0,128	-3,371	0,001
Women: $F_{totál}$=21,627; df=5/552; p<0,000			
Pleasure of life	0,398	4,734	0,000
Positive attitude towards life	0,302	5,874	0,000
Depressive mood	-0,225	-3,465	0,000
Personal prob-lems	-0,184	-3,265	0,000
Somatic symp-toms and reac-tions	-0,187	-4,516	0,000
Men: $F_{totál}$=11,298; df=3/302; p<0,000			
Positive attitude towards life	0,467	4,852	0,000
Pleasure of life	0,385	4,657	0,000
Depressive mood a	-0257	-2,763	0,008

Chart 3. The regression of the results scored on the Spiritual Consciousness Scale on the various scales measuring subjective well-being (approved models; p<0,05)

In the examination, the results achieved on the Spiritual Consciousness Scale were the dependent variables and the various components of subjective well-being were the predictors (Chart 3).

In the entire sample, a significant and positive interrelation was observed between the Spiritual Consciousness and positive attitude toward life and joy of life on the scales measuring subjective well-being, and a considerably negative correlation with depressive mood and personal problems that together amounted to 12,4% of the variance of spiritual consciousness.

As far as differences between the two genders are concerned, the various components of subjective well-being explain 11,9% of the variance of the Spiritual Consciousness in women.

A significant positive connection with the joy of life and a positive attitude to life was observed, whereas a similarly significant negative relationship with a depressive mood, personal problems and somatic symptoms and reactions was recorded. In the case of men, 12,9% of the variance of spiritual Consciousness is determined by various components of subjective well-being.

These components were found to be in a close positive correlation with a positive attitude toward life and the joy of life, and in a negative correlation with a depressive mood.

Discussion

In subjective well-being - in accordance with our initial - did not observe any considerable difference. The only exceptions to that were identified in somatic symptoms and reactions, as women were found to be more susceptible to these reactions than men. These results are in full harmony with the findings of other research programmes (Diener et al., 1999). The results of our research also confirmed our second hypothesis, that is, students with higher Spiritual Consciousness also have a higher subjective well-being than those at a lower level of Spiritual Consciousness.

The research project proved that students at a high level of Spiritual Consciousness reported a significantly higher level of subjective well-being and had significantly fewer somatic complaints and symptoms and fewer personal problems than the students who did not yet have Spiritual Consciousness. The withdrawal of the functions of the Ego and the emergence of the alert consciousness in the present tend to increase the subjective well-being of the individual, who becomes more resistant to the personal problems and physical reactions generated by the Ego's survival mode.

Our third hypothesis was confirmed as well. The assumption was that among the students with a high Spiritual Consciousness, there were not any considerable differences in subjective well-being between the genders.

Our fourth hypothesis—that there was a close correlation between the Spiritual Consciousness and certain indicators of subjective well-being—also proved to be true. In both sexes, the Spiritual Consciousness was in a significant positive correlation with a positive attitude toward life and the joy of life, and in a significant negative correlation with depressive moods. In personal problems and somatic symptoms, we found that the Spiritual Consciousness is able to reduce the susceptibility to these reactions in women more than in the case of men.

Individual Aspirations and Spirituality

Introduction

In Emmons's theory personality is interpreted as a motivation system, in which the emphasis is on the personal objectives (or system of objectives) that drive human behaviour and on the achievement of the objectives (Emmons, 1986).

The research conducted by Emmons and Diener (1985) suggest that individuals who regard their own actions as ones that do not generate conflicts tend to be more satisfied with life.

Diener and Fujita (1995), in another examination that they carried out in order to study the interrelations of personal goals, social and internal resources and well-being/satisfaction with life, found that social and internal resources have a considerable effect on satisfaction with life. Non-social external resources (e.g., material goods, money) do not appear to influence emotional well-being, but they correlate with satisfaction with life to a medium extent. Furthermore, an examination of the individual patterns of various resources revealed differences between men and women. Women find social objectives such as emotional control and social skills, including the resources required for achieving these goals, more important than men do. The system of objectives of men, on the other hand, largely contains performance objectives like authority, achievements in sports and knowledge acquired through experience. The resources leading to these goals are primarily performance and instrumental means.

Kasser and Ryan (1993), when examining the connections among values, objectives and subjective well-being, found that individuals giving priority to extrinsic goals (their endeavours are focused on financial success, the acquisition of material goods) demonstrated a generally lower well-being and a worse psychological situation, regardless of their gender, than those for whom intrinsic goals (self-acceptance, social relations and social commitments) were more important.

The research programmes conducted by Kasser and Ryan (1996), as well as other researchers, among people of various ages and social backgrounds (lower, middle and upper classes) in cultures different from that of the U.S., suggest that there is a reverse proportion between the attribution of great importance to material values and subjective well-being. The studies mentioned above justify the theories of humanistic thinkers that for subjective well-being, intrinsic objectives are more central than extrinsic ones.

Research Hypotheses

Our initial research hypotheses were the following:

1. For college students (in accordance with the representative samples from Hungary), intrinsic objectives, particularly health, personal advancement and social relations are the most important.

2. In terms of personal aspirations, there will be considerable differences between the two genders, with women attributing greater significance to the intrinsic

aspirations and image and men regarding wealth as more important.

3. As for intrinsic aspirations, women will find health and social relations the most important, while men will tend to ascribe the greatest importance to personal advancement.

4. Students with a higher level of Spiritual Consciousness ascribed much less importance to both intrinsic and extrinsic individual aspirations than those at a lower grade of Spiritual Consciousness.

5. In terms of individual aspirations, there are no gender differences between the students possessing a high degree of Spiritual Consciousness.

6. There appears to be a close correlation between the Spiritual Consciousness and certain indicators of individual aspirations.

Methodology

Participants

The sample participating in the examination was the same as described in Chapter 1.

Measures

Examination of Individual Aspirations

Aspiration Inventory

The self-determination theory of Deci and Ryan (1985, 2000) constitutes the theoretical foundation of the questionnaire, according to which the sound functioning, growth and inner integration of a personality is primarily driven by the efforts to satisfy certain innate and universal needs. The authors identify three of these needs as elementary: the individual's desire for autonomy, the individual's desire for positive relations and an ability for competent, independent action. These basic needs serve as the major motivating forces of the personality. It is possible to satisfy these needs through self-motivation (intrinsic motives) and external motivation (extrinsic motives). The authors revealed the most characteristic intrinsic and extrinsic motives through empirical research. The motives were formulated in the form of aspirations, objectives in life.

The Aspiration Inventory (Kasser and Ryan, 1996) is a means of revealing long-term objectives and aspirations; it contains a total of 35 aspirations (objective, motive), clustered around 7 categories of goals in life, represented by the 7 scales of the questionnaire.

Five items belong to each of the 7 scales. These are the following:

> Wealth
> Reputation
> Image (good appearance)
> Growth (personal advancement)
> Social relations (good personal con-
  nections)
> Society (social commitment)
> Health

Respondents are supposed to judge the aspirations listed in the questionnaire according to three aspects on a seven-grade

Likert-scale:

> Importance (How important is the objective concerned for you?)
> Probability (What is the likelihood of this happening to you in the future?)
> Realization (How much of the objective above have you been able to achieve?)

The most important extrinsic motivations (aspirations): wealth, reputation and image. The primary intrinsic motivations (aspirations): personal advancement, social relations and social commitment. Kasser and Ryan (1996) assert that health does not clearly belong to any of the aspirations. In compliance with the findings of several international research programmes,

Komlósi et al. (2006), as a result of a survey in Hungary, listed health with the intrinsic aspirations. In the course of the Hungarian adaptation of the questionnaire, Komlósi et al. (2006) found the reliability of the dimensions excellent (Cronbach-alpha=0,72-0,91).

Examination of Spiritual Consciousness

The Spiritual Consciousness Scale (Margitics, 2019)

The questionnaire describes the following dimensions of Spiritual Consciousness:

> - Transcending the Functions of Ego
> - Ego-Dyastole (reduction in the functions of Ego)
> - Alert Consciousness in the Present

Results

The descriptive and comparative statistics of Aspiration Inventory are summarized in Chart 1.

In the whole sample, when the importance of the various aspirations was examined, the highest values were measured in health, personal advancement and social relations. Most respondents found these aspirations extremely important, which is also indicated by the fact the dispersion was the smallest in health and social relations (the large standard deviation found in personal growth, on the other hand, indicates the large personal differences at this point).

Aspiration Inventory	Total (n=854)	
	Mean Value	Standard Deviation
Wealth: importance	22,7	5,5
Wealth: probability	19,5	5,1
Wealth: realization	15,2	5,5
Reputation: importance	17,1**	7,3
Reputation: probability	15***	5,9
Reputation: realization	11,5***	5
Image: importance	23,2***	6,7
Image: probability	21,5***	5,9
Image: realization	19,3*	6,3
Personal advancement: importance	31,8	13,2
Personal advancement:	26,6*	4,7

probability		
Personal advancement: realization	21,7	5,5
Personal relationships: importance	32,1***	3,2
Personal relationships: probability	28,8***	4,7
Personal relationships: realization	24,9***	9,4
Social commitment: importance	25,2*	5,8
Social commitment: probability	22,8**	5,7
Social commitment: realization	16,5	6,1
Health: importance	32,8***	3,4
Health: probability	26,3***	5,5
Health: realization	23,5*	6,5
Intrinsic: importance	123,5***	11,5
Intrinsic: probability	103,1***	16,8
Intrinsic: realization	87,2**	19,7

	Mean Value	Standard Deviation
Extrinsic: importance	65,2	17,4
Extrinsic: probability	57,1	14,5
Extrinsic: realization	46,8	14,2
Aspiration Inventory	Women (n=552)	
	Mean Value	Standard Deviation
Wealth: importance	23,8	5,7
Wealth: probability	19,5	5
Wealth: realization	15,2	5,4
Reputation: importance	16,7	7,2
Reputation: probability	14,6	5,7
Reputation: realization	11,3	4,7
Image: importance	24	6,6
Image: probability	21,9	5,8
Image: realization	19,6	6,2
Personal advancement: importance	30,9	8,4
Personal ad-	27,1	4,5

vancement: probability		
Personal advancement: realization	22	5,5
Personal relationships: importance	32,3	2,8
Personal relationships: probability	29	4,2
Personal relationships: realization	25,8	9,4
Social commitment: importance	25,4	5,6
Social commitment: probability	22,7	5,6
Social commitment: realization	17	6
Health: importance	32,7	2,9
Health: probability	26,8	5,3
Health: realization	23,6	6,5
Intrinsic: importance	123,8	10,7
Intrinsic: probability	104,9	14,9
Intrinsic: realiza-	88,3	19,7

	Mean Value	Standard Deviation
tion		
Extrinsic: importance	59,7	17,4
Extrinsic: probability	57,3	14
Extrinsic: realization	46,9	13,8
Aspiration Inventory	Men (n=302)	
	Mean Value	Standard Deviation
Wealth: importance	24,3	5,6
Wealth: probability	20,1	5,5
Wealth: realization	15,2	5,8
Reputation: importance	18,6	7,7
Reputation: probability	16,8	6,4
Reputation: realization	13,1	5,6
Image: importance	20,7	6,7
Image: probability	19,5	6,1
Image: realization	18,5	6,5
Personal advancement: importance	32,1	23,1

Personal advancement: probability	26	5
Personal advancement: realization	21,1	5,6
Personal relationships: importance	30,1	4,4
Personal relationships: probability	26,5	5,6
Personal relationships: realization	22,8	7,2
Social commitment: importance	24,6	6,4
Social commitment: probability	21	5,9
Social commitment: realization	16	6,1
Health: importance	31	4,5
Health: probability	24,3	6,1
Health: realization	22,8	6,7
Intrinsic: importance	118,3	14,3
Intrinsic: probability	98,9	18,9

Intrinsic: realization	83,2	20,8
Extrinsic: importance	65,1	15,9
Extrinsic: probability	56,4	14,8
Extrinsic: realization	46,5	15,8

*p<0,05; **p<0,01; ***p<0,001.

Chart 1. The descriptive and comparative statistics of Aspiration Inventory

The least important goals in life for the respondents were the three extrinsic aspirations: reputation, wealth and image. Intrinsic aspirations are, therefore, favoured by college students over the extrinsic ones.

These findings largely coincide with the results obtained by Komlósi et al. (2006) as a result of their examination conducted on a representative sample (with the exception of the value of standard deviation found at personal growth, which was larger in their sample).

Szondy (2004) also found intrinsic aspirations more characteristic in his sample of late adolescent age (average age: 17,38 years).

The order of importance of the aspirations was the following: social relations, health, and personal growth, followed by social responsibility. The adolescents also listed extrinsic aspirations with the least important ones, in the order of wealth, image and, finally, reputation.

If we examine the order of importance, we find the intrinsic aspirations on the top of the lists in both genders, with smaller shifts in emphasis. While the order of importance for women is health, social relations and personal advancement, men place personal advancement in the first position, followed by health and social relations. Social commitment is the fourth in the list of both genders.

On the list of women, it is followed by image and wealth, with approximately the same values, whereas wealth precedes image on the list of men. Reputation is the last on the lists of both sexes. Our findings in connection with the extrinsic aspirations match those of Komlósi et al. (2006) obtained from their survey of a representative sample.

They found health as the most important intrinsic aspiration in both genders, followed by social relations on the list of women, and personal growth on the list of men.

The comparative statistical analysis (two paired t-test) suggests that women scored considerably higher in the combined index of intrinsic aspirations, health, social relations, image and social commitment. Men, on the other hand, gave higher points to reputation.

Szondy (2004) also observed this difference between the two sexes, except the higher value of reputation on the list of men. No considerable difference was observed between the two genders at the combined index of extrinsic aspirations, personal growth and wealth.

These findings only partially match the results obtained by Komlósi et al. (2006) from their representative sample. In their findings, men scored significantly higher in their aspiration for wealth, whereas women scored considerably higher in image, personal advancement, social relations, social commitment and health than men did.

In an examination of the entire sample from the aspect of the probability of the various aspirations, the highest values were also measured at the intrinsic aspirations, in the order of social relations, personal advancement and health. They are followed by the extrinsic aspirations, in the order of the image, wealth and reputation.

Szondy (2004) found the same order in late adolescent age. An examination of the order or probability according to the two genders, we find the same tendency in women. In men, there is only one deviation, as they place wealth before image. In the probability of various aspirations, we found similar differences to those observed at the degree of importance. The only exception was that women gave considerably greater emphasis to personal advancement.

When analysing the realization of the aspirations in the whole sample, the highest values are observed in the intrinsic aspirations. The order is the following: social relations, health and personal growth. The fourth one is an extrinsic aspiration, image, followed by social commitment, wealth and reputation. This was the order in both genders.

In connection with realization, Szondy (2004) found a similar pattern among adolescents, with slight changes in emphasis: health, social relations, personal advancement, image, social responsibility, wealth and reputation. In the probability of various aspirations, we found similar differences to those observed in the degree of importance. The only exception to that was that no significant difference between the two genders was observable in terms of the realization of social commitment.

Unfortunately, we did not have an opportunity to compare the probability and realization of the various aspirations with the representative sample, as Komlósi et al. (2006) did not provide relevant data in their study.

Figure 1 contains the descriptive statistics of the results scored on the Aspiration Inventory by the examination groups created according to the Spiritual Consciousness Scale. The results are arranged in the order of priorities identified by the participants.

The figures suggest that, regardless of their gender, students scoring lower in the Spiritual Consciousness Scale and possesing a lower level of spiritual consciousness reported a higher level of importance of both intrinsic and extrinsic personal aspirations. Students with a higher level of Spiritual Consciousness, on the other hand, ascribed a smaller importance to interinsic and extrinsic aspirations (intrinsic: t=4,143, p<0,000; extrinsic: t=7,803, p<0,000).

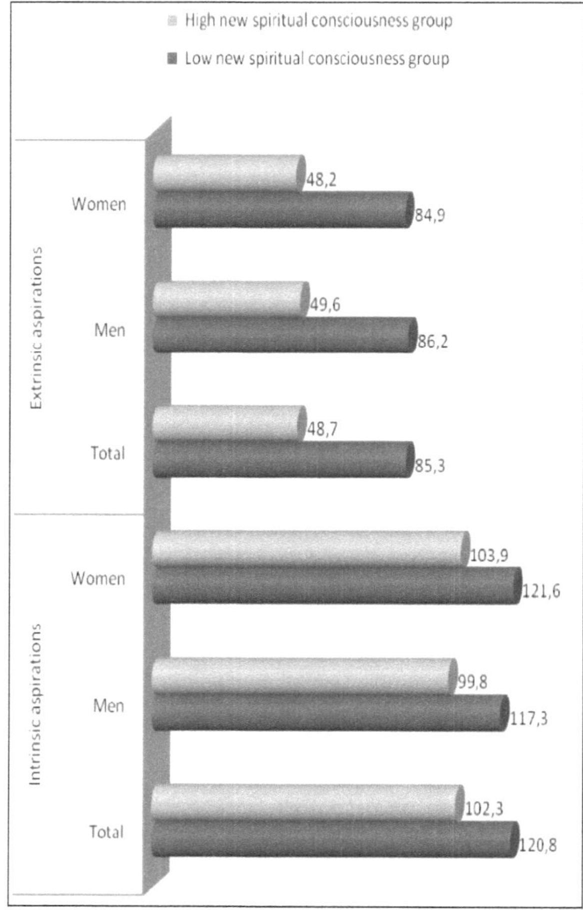

Figure 1. The mean average results of the priorities identified in the Aspiration Inventory by the members of the groups created according to their scrores in the Spiritual Consciousness Scale.

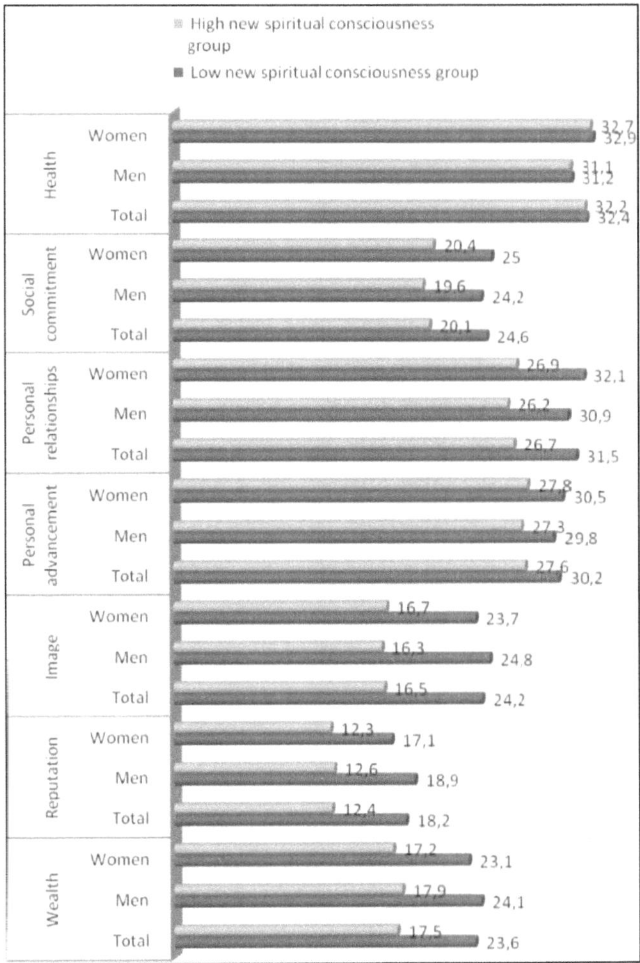

Figure 2. The scores achieved at certain scales of the Aspiration Inventory (importance) in the groups created according to the results scored at the Spiritual Consciousness Scale.

It was examined what differences were observable between the two examination groups in terms of the importance of intrinsic and extrinsic aspirations (Figure 2).

The only category of the personal intrinsic aspirations at which no considerable difference was revealed between the two groups was health. Students with a lower level of Spiritual Consciousness attributed more importance to personal advancement, good social relations and social commitments than those with a higher level of spiritual Consciousness. According to the comparative statistical analysis of these results, the differences were significant (personal advancement: t=5,593, p<0,000; personal relationships: t=4,832, p<0,000; social commitment: t=3,262, p<0,000).

In all three scales of extrinsic personal aspirations (wealth, reputation and image) students with a lower level of spiritual Consciousness also tended to score higher (wealth: t=8,543, p<0,000; image: t=7,322, p<0,000; reputation: t=4,656, p<0,000).

Figure 3 contains the descriptive statistics of the results scored on the Aspiration Inventory by the examination groups created according to the Spiritual Consciousness Scale.

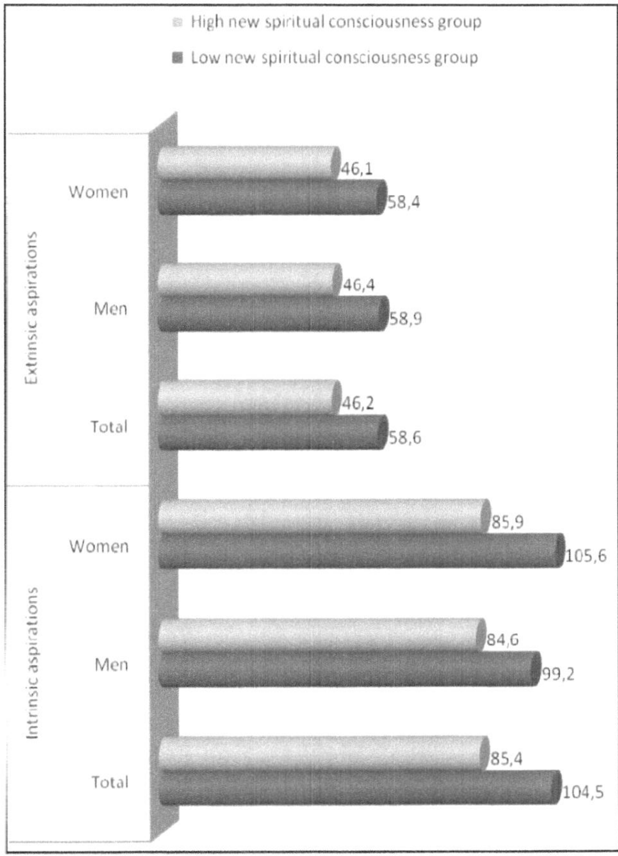

Figure 3. The mean average results of the probability identified in the Aspiration Inventory by the members of the groups created according to their scrores in the Spiritual Consciousness Scale.

The results are arranged in the order of probability identified by the participants.

The figures suggest that, regardless of their gender, students scoring lower in the Spiritual Consciousness Scale and possesing a lower level of spiritual consciousness reported a higher level of probability of both intrinsic and extrinsic personal aspirations. Students with a higher level of Spiritual Consciousness, on the other hand, ascribed a smaller importance to interinsic and extrinsic aspirations (intrinsic: t=4,598, p<0,000; extrinsic: t=6,972, p<0,000)

It was examined what differences were observable between the two examination groups in terms of the probability of intrinsic and extrinsic aspirations (Figure 4).

When examining the probability of the individual personal aspirations, we were able to identify the same tendency as what we had found when analysing the importance of the individual aspirations (intrinsic aspirations: personal advancement: t=5,145, p<0,000; personal relationships: t=4,752, p<0,000; social commitment: t=3,112, p<0,000; extrinsic aspirations: wealth: t=6,444, p<0,000; image: t=6,312, p<0,000; reputation: t=4,136, p<0,000).

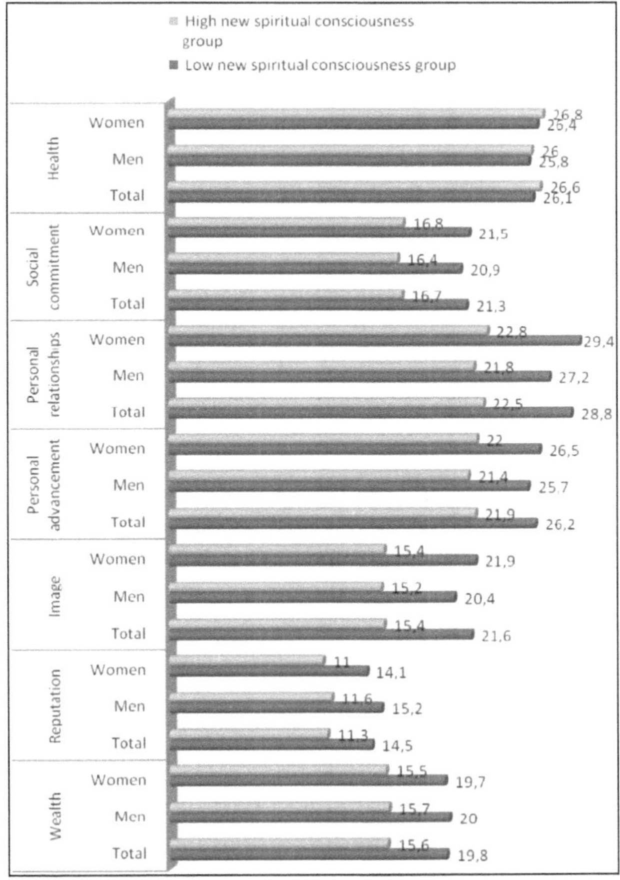

Figure 4. The scores achieved at certain scales of the Aspiration Inventory (probability) in the groups created according to the results scored at the Spiritual Consciousness Scale.

Figure 5 contains the descriptive statistics of the results scored on the Aspiration Inventory by the examination groups created according to the Spiritual Consciousness Scale. The results are arranged in the order of realization identified by the participants.

The figure indicates that there is no considerable difference betweeen the two groups in terms of the realization of the intrinsic and extrinsic aspirations. It equally applies to both genders.

It was examined what differences were observable between the two examination groups in terms of the realization of intrinsic and extrinsic aspirations.

No considerable difference was revealed between the two groups in terms of the realization of the individual aspirations.

In the subsequent part of the research, a linear regression analysis (stepwise method) of the various components of the individual aspirations was carried out for the entire sample and for the two genders separately. In this research, the dependent variable was the result scored on the Spiritual Consciousness Scale, whereas the individual components of the individual aspirations were used as predictor (Chart 2).

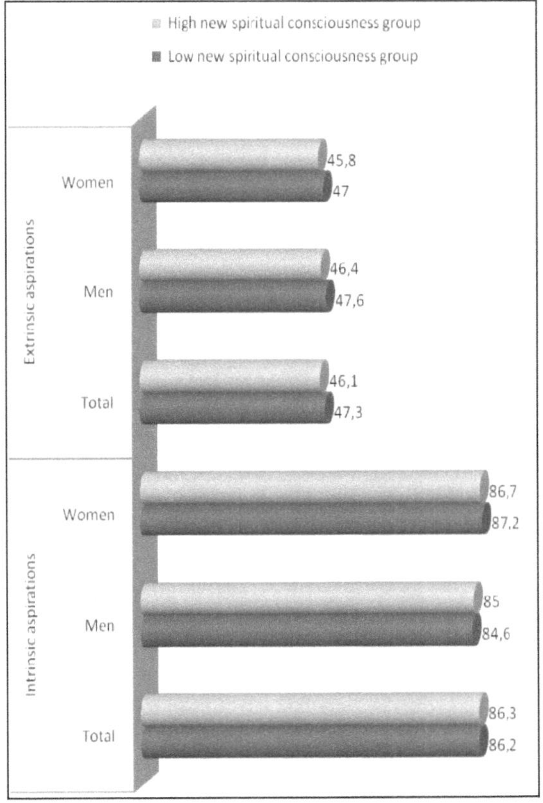

Figure 5. The mean average results of the realization identified in the Aspiration Inventory by the members of the groups created according to their scrores in the Spiritual Consciousness Scale.

Prediktor	β	t	p<
Total: F_{total}=27,873; df=2/854; p<0,000			
Personal advancement: realization	-0,192	-0,5,247	0,000
Social commitment: importance	-0,162	-4,416	0,000
Women: F_{total}=22,252; df=2/552; p<0,000			
Personal advancement: realization	-0,200	-4,765	0,000
Social commitment: importance	-0,156	-3,702	0,000
Men: F_{total}=21,5228; df=2/302; p<0,000			
Personal advancement: realization	-0,186	-4,451	0,000
Social commitment: importance	-0,142	-3,147	0,000

Chart 2. The regression of the results scored at the Spiritual Consciousness Scale to various scales of the questionnaire measuring individual aspirations (approved models; p<0,05)

In the entire sample, there was a significant negative correlation between the Spiritual Consciousness and accomplished personal advancement and the importance of social commitment out of the scales measuring individual aspirations. The correlation with these items amount to 7,4% of the variance of the Spiritual Consciousness.

This was the same in both genders (significant negative connection with accomplished personal advancement and the importance of social commitment), explaining 7,5% of the variance of the Spiritual Consciousness in women, and 6,7% in men.

Discussion

In our first hypothesis, the prevalence of individual aspirations, we had assumed that—similar to the results of the research of Komlósi et al. (2006) conducted on a representative Hungarian sample college students would find intrinsic objectives, and within those, health, personal relations and social relations the most important.

Our research findings suggest that college students also tend to favour intrinsic aspirations over the extrinsic aspirations. In compliance with the findings of Komlósi et al. (2006), college students found health, personal growth and social relations the most important personal aspirations. The found the extrinsic aspirations, reputation, wealth and image as the least important objectives in life.

We have also been able to confirm our second initial hypothesis, that is, there would be a considerable difference between the genders in terms of individual aspirations, as women would find image, whereas men would find wealth as important goals in life, as suggested by the findings of Komlósi et al. (2006) earlier. In the sample of college students, however, men—unlike earlier findings with Hungarian samples—gave priority to reputation over wealth, which is different from the list of importance set up by women.

In research conducted in Hungary by V. Komlósi et al. [6], it was found that women put social relations directly after health on the list of intrinsic aspirations, whereas for men, the most important ambition was personal growth.

Our third hypothesis was that it was going to be the same with college students. We found the domination of intrinsic aspirations in both genders, with only slight shifts of emphasis. For women, health, social relations and personal growth was the order, for men, personal advancement was on the top of the list, followed by health and social relations. These results are in full compliance with the results of Komlósi et al. (2006).

Our fourth hypothesis, that is, students with a higher degree of Spiritual Consciousness would score lower at judging the importance and likelihood of both the intrinsic and extrinsic individual aspirations than students with a lower level of Spiritual Consciousness would, was also verified.

Personal aspirations are closely linked to the functions of the Ego; these are, in fact, the efforts of the Ego to extend and reinforce itself.

In individuals with a high degree of Spiritual Consciousness, however, the withdrawal of the functions of the Ego is observable, as the individual overcomes the functions of the Ego. As a consequence, the personal aspirations, both intrinsic and extrinsic, tend to loose some of their original importance.

Our fifth hypothesis, the lack of gender differences among students with a high Spiritual Consciousness in terms of individual aspirations, was also confirmed. Tolle (1997, 2006) asserts that the development of conscience is independent of gender.

We were also able to confirm our sixth hypothesis, according to which there was a close correlation between the Spiritual Consciousness and certain indicators of personal aspirations.

The Spiritual Consciousness was found to be in a close connection primarily with the lack of personal advancement and the importance of social commitment. It may suggest that the Spiritual Consciousness may appear in individuals who are not satisfied with the present level of their personal advancement and seek unconventional methods of personal advancement and progress.

References

Brebner, J., Donaldson, J., Kirby, N., Ward, L. (1995). Relationship between happiness and personality. *Personality and Individual Differences, 19*, 251-258.

Brunstein, J.C. (1993). Personal goals and subjective well-being: a longitudinal study. *Journal of Personality and Social Psychology, 65*, 1061-1070.

Chan, R., and Joseph, S. (2000). Dimensions of personality, domains of aspirations, and subjective well-being. *Personality and Individual Differences, 28*, 347-354.

Deci, E. L., and Ryan, R. M. (1985). Intrinsic Motivation and Self-determination in Human Behavior. New York: Plenum.

Deci, E. L.,and Ryan, R. M. (2000). The "what" and "why" of goal pursuits: human needs and the self-determination of behaviour. *Psychological Inquiry, 11*, 227-268.

Diener, E., Such, E.M., Lucas, R.E., & Smith, H.L. (1999). Subjective well-being: three decades of progress. *Psychology Bulletin, 125,* 276-302.

Diener, E. (2000). Subjective well-being: the science of happiness and a proposal for a national index. *American Psychologist, 55*, 34-43.

Diener, E., and Fujita (1995). Recources, personal strivings, and subjective well-being: a nomothetic and idiographic approach. *Journal of Personality and Social Psychology, 68,* 926-935.

Emmons, R. A. (1986). Personal strivings: an approach to personality and subjective well-being. *Journal of Personality and Social Psychology, 51*, 1058-1068.

Emmons, R.A., and Diener, E. (1985): Personality correlates of subjective well-being. *Personality and Social Psychology Bulletin, 11*, 89-97.

Grob, A. (1995). Subjective well-being and significant life-events across the life-span. *Swiss Journal of Psychology, 54*, 3-18.

Lu, L., and Shih, J.B. (1997). Personality and happiness: is mental health a mediator? *Personality and Individual Differences, 22*, 249-256.

Kasser, T., and Ryan, R.M. (1993). A dark side of the American dream: correlates of financial success as a central life aspiration. *Journal of Personality and Social Psychology, 65*, 410-422.

Kasser, T., and Ryan, R.M. (1996), Further examining the American dream: differential correlates of intrinsic and extrinsic goals. *Personality and Social Psychology Bulletin, 22,* 280-287.

Komlósi, A., Rózsa S., Bérdi M., Móricz É., Horváth D. (2006). Az Aspirációs Index hazai alkalmazásával szerzett tapasztalatok. *Magyar Pszichológiai Szemle, 61,* 237-250.

Margitics F. (2019): The Spiritual Consciousness Scale /Handbook/. KeryPub, New York.

Martos, T., Szabó G., Rózsa S. (2006). Az Aspirációs Index rövidített változatának pszichometriai jellemzői hazai mintán. *Mentálhigiéné és Pszichoszomatika, 7,* 171-191.

Sallay, H. (2004): Entering the job market: belief in a just wordl, fairness and well-being of graduation students. In C. Dalbert, and H. Sallay (Eds.), *The Justice Motive in Adolescence and Young Adulthood: Origins and Consequences* (pp. 215-231). Routledge, London: Routledge.

Szondy, M. (2004). A szubjektív jóllét és a törekvések kapcsolata késői serdülőkorban. *Alkalmazott Pszichológia, 4,* 53-72.

Urbán, R. (1995). Boldogság, személyiség és egészség. [Happiness, personality and health.] *Magyar Pszichológiai Szemle, 35,* 379-404.

PREVIOUS BOOK:

https://www.amazon.com/dp/B07VWJMQ7X

9 781711 735689